Descendants of Robert Bowie

Generation 1

1. **ROBERT**[1] **BOWIE** was born on 11 Nov 1761 in Ormiston, East Lothian, Scotland. He married Euphemia Simson, daughter of John Simson and Beatrix Cunningham on 08 Jan 1779 in Tranent, East Lothian, Scotland. She was born on 03 Sep 1757 in Tranent, East Lothian, Scotland.

    Robert Bowie and Euphemia Simson had the following children:

    i.   ANN[2] BOWIE was born on 21 Nov 1779 in Tranent, East Lothian, Scotland.

3. ii. ALEXANDER BOWIE was born on 14 Jul 1786 in Pencaitland, East Lothian, Scotland. He died on 02 Jun 1841 in Newbattle, Scotland. He married Isabel Bernard, daughter of James Bernard and Margaret Bannerman on 24 May 1811 in Liberton, Midlothian, Scotland. She was born about 1791 in Halbeath, Dunfermline, Scotland. She died on 06 Mar 1860 in Whitehill, Midlothian, Scotland.

    iii. JOHN BOWIE was born on 02 Aug 1789 in Renfrew, Renfrewshire, Scotland.

3. iv. HUNTER BOWIE was born on 08 May 1795 in Muirkirk, Ayr, Scotland. He died on 17 Mar 1844 in Loanhead, Midlothian, Scotland. He married Isabella Walker Craig, daughter of Robert Craig and Euphan Kinghorn on 25 Dec 1813 in Lasswade, Midlothian, Scotland. She was born on 28 Sep 1788 in Newton, Midlothian, Scotland. She died on 14 Aug 1879 in Hunterfield Stobhill, Midlothian, Scotland.

    v.   MARION BOWIE was born on 10 Dec 1797 in Muirkirk, Ayr, Scotland.

4. vi. EUPHEMIA BOWIE was born on 30 Jan 1800 in Muirkirk, Ayr, Scotland. She married (1) ALEXANDER HISLOP on 14 Nov 1825 in St. Cuthberts, Edinburgh, Midlothian, Scotland. She married (UNKNOWN).

Generation 2

2. **ALEXANDER**[2] **BOWIE** (Robert[1]) was born on 14 Jul 1786 in Pencaitland, East Lothian, Scotland. He died on 02 Jun 1841 in Newbattle, Scotland. He married Isabel Bernard, daughter of James Bernard and Margaret Bannerman on 24 May 1811 in Liberton, Midlothian, Scotland. She was born about 1791 in Halbeath, Dunfermline, Scotland. She died on 06 Mar 1860 in Whitehill, Midlothian, Scotland.

    Alexander Bowie and Isabel Bernard had the following children:

5. i.   JOHN[3] BOWIE was born on 13 Jan 1823 in Newton, Midlothian, Scotland. He died on 23 Jul 1875 in Hickory, Mercer County, Pennsylvania. He married Catherine Neilson, daughter of Joseph Neilson and Catherine Mathieson on 21 Sep 1844 in Newbattle, Midlothian, Scotland. She was born on 11 Jun 1823 in Huntershall, Midlothian, Scotland. She died after 11 Jun 1900.

6. ii. JAMES BOWIE was born in 1812 in Lasswade, Midlothian, Scotland. He married Jean Neilson, daughter of Joseph Neilson and Catherine Mathieson on 13 Jan 1837 in Newbattle, Midlothian, Scotland. She was born on 03 Sep 1812 in Huntershall, Scotland.

7. iii. MARGARET BOWIE was born about 1817 in Lasswade, Midlothian, Scotland. She died after 12 Jun 1880. She married John Laing on 20 Jan 1838 in Gave their names for proclamation in Newbattle, Midlothian, Scotland. He was born about 1817 in Lasswade, Midlothian, Scotland. He died after 12 Jun 1880.

8. iv. EUPHEMIA BOWIE was born about 1821 in Newton, Midlothian, Scotland. She died on 22 Sep 1856 in Newtongrange, Scotland. She married THOMAS DAVIDSON. He

born about 1820. He died after Sep 1856.

9.   v. ISABEL BOWIE was born on 12 Nov 1826 in Newton, Midlothian, Scotland. She married Alexander Sommerville on 08 Aug 1846 in Newbattle, Midlothian, Scotland. He was born about 1824 in Edinburgh, Midlothian, Scotland.

10.   vi. HUNTER BOWIE was born on 03 Oct 1830 in Newton, Midlothian, Scotland. He died in 1907 in Mercer County, Pennsylvania. He married Margaret Baillie Neilson, daughter of Joseph Neilson and Catherine Mathieson about 1854. She was born on 16 Sep 1829 in Liberton, Midlothian, Scotland. She died in 1906.

3.   **HUNTER**[2] **BOWIE** (Robert[1]) was born on 08 May 1795 in Muirkirk, Ayr, Scotland. He died on 17 Mar 1844 in Loanhead, Midlothian, Scotland. He married Isabella Walker Craig, daughter of Robert Craig and Euphan Kinghorn on 25 Dec 1813 in Lasswade, Midlothian, Scotland. She was born on 28 Sep 1788 in Newton, Midlothian, Scotland. She died on 14 Aug 1879 in Hunterfield Stobhill, Midlothian, Scotland.

More About Hunter Bowie:
Occupation: Coal Miner

Hunter Bowie and Isabella Walker Craig had the following children:

11.   i. EUPHEMIA[3] BOWIE was born on 31 Jan 1814 in Loanhead, Midlothian, Scotland. She died on 30 Mar 1902 in Waratah, NSW, Australia. She married William Smith, son of Robert Smith and Mary Campbell on 03 Mar 1833 in Lasswade, Midlothian, Scotland. He was born on 04 Nov 1813 in Lasswade, Midlothian, Scotland. He died about 1851 in Lasswade, Midlothian, Scotland.

      ii. CHRISTIAN BOWIE was born on 20 Oct 1816 in Lasswade, Midlothian, Scotland.

          More About Christian Bowie:
          Occupation: Coal Bearer

      iii. ELIZABETH BOWIE was born in 1821 in Lasswade, Midlothian, Scotland.

      iv. CHRISTIAN BOWIE was born in 1823 in Lasswade, Midlothian, Scotland.

      v. MARY BOWIE was born on 01 Mar 1825 in Liberton, Midlothian, Scotland.

12.   vi. ROBERT BOWIE was born on 05 Mar 1827 in Lasswade, Midlothian, Scotland. He died on 27 Apr 1911. He married Mary Young, daughter of Thomas Young and Marion Neilson on 09 Sep 1848 in Lasswade, Midlothian, Scotland. She was born on 06 Feb 1830 in Hunterfield, Midlothian, Scotland. She died on 06 Nov 1902 in Hunterfield, Midlothian, Scotland.

      vii. CATHERINE BOWIE was born on 01 Jul 1829 in Lasswade, Midlothian, Scotland.

      viii. ANN BOWIE was born about 1831 in Lasswade, Midlothian, Scotland.

      ix. DAVID BOWIE was born on 26 Mar 1833 in Lassawade, Midlothian, Scotland.

      x. ALEXANDER BOWIE was born on 06 Feb 1835 in Lasswade, Midlothian, Scotland.

More About Alexander Bowie:
Occupation: Coal Miner

4.   EUPHEMIA^2 BOWIE (Robert^1) was born on 30 Jan 1800 in Muirkirk, Ayr, Scotland. She married (1) ALEXANDER HISLOP on 14 Nov 1825 in St. Cuthberts, Edinburgh, Midlothian, Scotland. She married (UNKNOWN).

Alexander Hislop and Euphemia Bowie had the following children:

13.   i. MARION AUCHETERLONIE^3 HISLOP was born on 28 Aug 1828 in Lasswade, Midlothian, Scotland. She married John Stewart on 31 Dec 1849 in Old Monkland, Lanarkshire, Scotland. He was born about 1826 in Sorby, Wigtonshire, Scotland.

           ii.   HURSTAN HISLOP was born in 1835 in Lasswade, Midlothian, Scotland.

           iii.   JAMES HISLOP was born in 1838 in Lasswade, Midlothian, Scotland.

(unknown) and Euphemia Bowie had the following child:

14.   i. ROBERT^3 BOWIE was born on 11 Nov 1821 in Lasswade, Midlothian, Scotland. He died on 16 Nov 1906 in Timaru, New Zealand. He married ANNE COLVILLE. She was born on 16 Oct 1820 in Shotts, Lanarkshire, Scotland. She died on 26 Aug 1899 in Timaru, New Zealand.

Generation 3

5.   JOHN^3 BOWIE (Alexander^2, Robert^1) was born on 13 Jan 1823 in Newton, Midlothian, Scotland. He died on 23 Jul 1875 in Hickory, Mercer County, Pennsylvania. He married Catherine Neilson, daughter of Joseph Neilson and Catherine Mathieson on 21 Sep 1844 in Newbattle, Midlothian, Scotland. She was born on 11 Jun 1823 in Huntershall, Midlothian, Scotland. She died after 11 Jun 1900.

More About John Bowie:
Burial: Keel Ridge Cemetery, Hermitage, Mercer County, Pennsylvania
Living In: 30 March 1851 Stobhill No. 67, Newbattle, Midlothian, Scotland
Occupation: 1851 in Newbattle, Midlothian, Scotland; Coal Miner
Occupation: 1860 in Hickory, Mercer County, Pennsylvania; Miner
Occupation: 1870 in Hickory Township, Mercer County, Pennsylvania; Coal Miner

More About Catherine Neilson:
Immigration: 1853 to Mercer County, Pennsylvania
Living In: 1880 South Hickory Township, Mercer County, Pennsylvania
Living In: 1900 Hickory Township, Mercer County, Pennsylvania

Notes for Catherine Neilson:
Arrived 22 August 1853 in New York, New York on sailing ship "Jessie Munn".

John Bowie and Catherine Neilson had the following children:

15.   i. CATHERINE^4 BOWIE was born on 28 Feb 1846 in Newbattle, Midlothian, Scotland. She died on 18 Aug 1923 in Grove City, Pennsylvania. She married George W. Crawford, son of Robert Crawford and Lillias Notman on 12 Apr 1862 in Sharon, Pennsylvania. He was born in 1840 in Scotland. He died on 22 Aug 1922 in Grove City, Pennsylvania.

16.   ii.   ISABELLA BOWIE was born in 1851 in Newbattle, Midlothian, Scotland. She died on

09 Jan 1891 in Pennsylvania. She married ROBERT VEITCH . He was born on 20 Nov 1839 in Edinbrurgh, Midlothian, Scotland. He died in 1900.

17.   iii. JANE BOWIE was born on 13 Jan 1853 in Sharon, Pennsylvania. She died on 26 Jun 1922 in Richland Grove, Mercer County, Illinois. She married William McNeil, son of John McNeil and Katherine Carr on 22 Dec 1871 in Sharon, Pennsylvania. He was born on 26 Mar 1844 in Tranent, East Lothian, Scotland. He died on 05 Mar 1918 in Griffin, Mercer County, Illinois.

18.   iv. MARGARET BOWIE was born on 25 Apr 1856 in Massilon, Stark County, Ohio. She died on 06 Aug 1943 in Krebs, Oklahoma. She married (1) DAVID ARCHIBALD about 1877. He was born in 1845 in Scotland. He died in May 1882 in Krebs, Indian Territory (Present Day Oklahoma). She married (2) PHILIP KEWLEY about 1890. He was born on 17 Jul 1846 in England. He died on 30 Nov 1931 in Pittsburg County, Oklahoma.

19.   v. ALEXANDER BOWIE was born about 22 Dec 1858 in Pennsylvania. He died on 04 Mar 1889 in McAlester, Indian Territory (Present Day Oklahoma). He married BARBARA PATTERSON BELL. She was born on 03 Mar 1867 in Silverbanks, Cambuslang, Lanarkshire, Scotland. She died on 12 Mar 1936 in Oklahoma City, Oklahoma.

20.   vi. ELLEN BOWIE was born in Apr 1861 in Mercer County, Pennsylvania. She died after 01 May 1940. She married John Lewis about 1882. He was born in Aug 1860 in England. He died between 16 Jan 1920-10 Apr 1930.

21.   vii. EUPHEMIA BOWIE was born on 25 Mar 1864 in Pennsylvania. She died on 02 May 1936 in Krebs, Pittsburg County, Oklahoma. She married John Evans, son of James Evans and Anna Harrison about 1880 in Hickory Township, Mercer County, Pennsylvania. He was born on 14 Sep 1859 in Pennsylvania. He died on 09 Mar 1942 in Pittsburg County, Oklahoma.

        viii. JENNET BOWIE was born in 1867 in Pennsylvania. She died in 1870.

        More About Jennet Bowie:
        Burial: Keel Ridge Cemetery, Hermitage, Mercer County, Pennsylvania

6.   **JAMES**[3] **BOWIE** (Alexander[2], Robert[1]) was born in 1812 in Lasswade, Midlothian, Scotland. He married Jean Neilson, daughter of Joseph Neilson and Catherine Mathieson on 13 Jan 1837 in Newbattle, Midlothian, Scotland. She was born on 03 Sep 1812 in Huntershall, Scotland.

More About James Bowie:
Immigration; to Mercer County, Pennsylvania
Occupation: Coal Miner

Notes for James Bowie:
Immigrated to Mercer County, Pennsylvania in 1862.

More About Jean Neilson:
Immigration: 1862 to Mercer County, Pennsylvania

James Bowie and Jean Neilson had the following children:

    i.   CATHERINE[4] BOWIE was born on 03 Feb 1838 in Cockpen, Midlothian, Scotland.

    ii.   ALEXANDER BOWIE was born on 23 Mar 1840 in Cockpen, Midlothian, Scotland.

    iii.   ELIZABETH BOWIE was born in 1842 in Cockpen, Midlothian, Scotland.

    iv.   JOSEPH BOWIE was born in 1844 in Cockpen, Midlothian, Scotland.

    v.   HELEN BOWIE was born in 1849 in Cockpen, Midlothian, Scotland.

    vi.   EUPHEMIA BOWIE was born in 1850 in Cockpen, Midlothian, Scotland. She married WALTER CUNNINGHAM.

    vii.   JOHN BOWIE was born in 1854 in Cockpen, Midlothian, Scotland.

7.   **MARGARET**[3] **BOWIE** (Alexander[2], Robert[1]) was born about 1817 in Lasswade, Midlothian, Scotland. She died after 12 Jun 1880. She married John Laing on 20 Jan 1838 in Gave their names for proclamation in Newbattle, Midlothian, Scotland. He was born about 1817 in Lasswade, Midlothian, Scotland. He died after 12 Jun 1880.

More About Margaret Bowie:
Immigration: 1867 to Mercer County, Pennsylvania

Notes for Margaret Bowie:
Arrived in New York, New York from Liverpool, England June 18, 1867 on ship "Tarifa".

More About John Laing:
Burial: Keel Ridge Cemetery, Hermitage, Mercer County, Pennsylvania
Immigration: 18 Jun 1867 to New York, New York
Occupation: 1870 in Hickory, Mercer County, Pennsylvania; Coal Miner
Occupation: 1880 in Hickory, Mercer County, Pennsylvania; Coal Miner

Notes for John Laing:
Arrived in New York, New York from Liverpool, England June 18, 1867 on ship "Tarifa".

John Laing and Margaret Bowie had the following children:

    i.   ISABELLA[4] LAING was born on 14 Jan 1839 in Newbattle, Midlothian, Scotland.

    ii.   ALEXANDER LAING was born on 21 Oct 1840 in Newbattle, Midlothian, Scotland. He married Elizabeth McAlpin, daughter of James McAlpin and Janet Morrison on 01 Apr 1864 in Slamannon, Stirling, Scotland. She was born on 09 Apr 1840 in Scotland. She died on 25 Oct 1929 in Cincinnati, Ohio.

    More About Alexander Laing:

    Notes for Alexander Laing:
    Arrived in New York, New York from Liverpool, England June 18, 1867 on ship "Tarifa".

iii.   ROBERT LAING was born on 01 Mar 1844 in Newbattle, Midlothian, Scotland. He married ANNIE (UNKNOWN).

More About Robert Laing:
Immigration: 18 Jun 1867 in New York, New York

Notes for Robert Laing:
Arrived, with his wife, in New York, New York from Liverpool, England June 18, 1867 on ship "Tarifa".

22.   iv. JAMES LAING was born on 02 Jan 1846 in Airdrie, Lanark, Scotland. He died on 31 Oct 1907 in Lewisburg, West Virginia. He married Susanna Kay, daughter of Thomas Kay and Janet Kerr on 31 Dec 1872. She was born on 29 Apr 1851 in Lanark, Scotland. She died on 30 Apr 1937 in Lewisburg, West Virginia.

v.   MARY LAING was born in 1849 in Slamannon, Stirling, Scotland.

More About Mary Laing:
Immigration: 18 Jun 1867 in New York, New York

Notes for Mary Laing:
Arrived, with her parents, in New York, New York from Liverpool, England June 18, 1867 on ship "Tarifa".

vi.   ANN LAING was born in 1851 in Linton, Scotland.

More About Ann Laing:
Immigration: 18 Jun 1867 in New York, New York

Notes for Ann Laing:
Arrived, with her parents, in New York, New York from Liverpool, England June 18, 1867 on ship "Tarifa".

vii.   JOHN LAING was born in 1854 in Slamannan, Stirling, Scotland. He married MARGARET (UNKNOWN). She was born about 1862.

More About John Laing:
Immigration: 18 Jun 1867 in New York, New York
Living In: 1880 John and Margaret are living with his parents in Hickory, Mercer County, Pennsylvania.
Occupation: 1870 in Hickory, Mercer County, Pennsylvania; Coal Miner
Occupation: 1880 in Hickory, Mercer County, Pennsylvania; Coal Miner

Notes for John Laing:
Arrived, with his parents, in New York, New York from Liverpool, England June 18, 1867 on ship "Tarifa".

    viii.   DAVID LAING was born on 03 Jan 1858 in Slamannan, Stirling, Scotland.

More About David Laing:
Immigration: 18 Jun 1867 in New York, New York

Notes for David Laing:
Arrived, with his parents, in New York, New York from Liverpool, England June 18, 1867 on ship "Tarifa".

    ix.   MARGARET LAING was born in 1868 in Pennsylvania.

8.   **EUPHEMIA^3 BOWIE** (Alexander^2, Robert^1) was born about 1821 in Newton, Midlothian, Scotland. She died on 22 Sep 1856 in Newtongrange, Scotland. She married **THOMAS DAVIDSON**. He was born about 1820. He died after Sep 1856.

Thomas Davidson and Euphemia Bowie had the following children:
    i.   ISABEL^4 DAVIDSON was born about 1842 in Newbattle, Scotland.

    ii.   ANNE DAVIDSON was born about 1845 in Newbattle, Scotland.

    iii.   JANE DAVIDSON was born about 1847 in Newbattle, Scotland.

9.   **ISABEL^3 BOWIE** (Alexander^2, Robert^1) was born on 12 Nov 1826 in Newton, Midlothian, Scotland. She married Alexander Sommerville on 08 Aug 1846 in Newbattle, Midlothian, Scotland. He was born about 1824 in Edinburgh, Midlothian, Scotland.

More About Isabel Bowie:
Immigration: 1851 to Mercer County, Pennsylvania

Notes for Isabel Bowie:
Immigrated to Mercer County, Pennsylvania.

More About Alexander Sommerville:
Immigration: 1851 to Mercer County, Pennsylvania

Alexander Sommerville and Isabel Bowie had the following children:
    i.   THOMAS^4 SOMMERVILLE was born about 1852 in Scotland.

    ii.   WILLIAM SOMMERVILLE was born about 1854 in Scotland.

    iii.   ALEXANDER SOMMERVILLE was born about 1856 in Pennsylvania.

iv.   JAMES B. SOMMERVILLE was born about 1858 in Pennsylvania.

v.   JOHN R. SOMMERVILLE was born about 1860 in Pennsylvania.

vi.   HUNTER SOMMERVILLE was born about 1862 in Pennsylvania.

vii.   WALTER SOMMERVILLE was born about 1865 in Pennsylvania.

viii.   EMMA SOMMERVILLE was born about 1868 in Pennsylvania.

10.   **HUNTER**[3] **BOWIE** (Alexander[2], Robert[1]) was born on 03 Oct 1830 in Newton, Midlothian, Scotland. He died in 1907 in Mercer County, Pennsylvania. He married Margaret Baillie Neilson, daughter of Joseph Neilson and Catherine Mathieson about 1854. She was born on 16 Sep 1829 in Liberton, Midlothian, Scotland. She died in 1906.

More About Hunter Bowie:
Immigration: 1852 to Mercer County, Pennsylvania
Occupation: 1860 in Hickory, Mercer County, Pennsylvania; Miner
Occupation: 1870 in Hickory Township, Mercer County, Pennsylvania; Coal Miner
Occupation: 1880 in South Hickory Township, Mercer County, Pennsylvania; Farmer
Occupation: 1900 in Hickory Township, Mercer County, Pennsylvania; Farmer

Notes for Hunter Bowie:
Immigrated to U. S. in 1852. Arrived in port of New York on October 5, 1852 aboard ship Affghan.

More About Margaret Baillie Neilson:
Immigration: 1853 to Mercer County,
Pennsylvania
Occupation: Lint Preparer

Hunter Bowie and Margaret Baillie Neilson had the following children:

i.   CATHERINE[4] BOWIE was born about 1855 in Pennsylvania.

24.   ii. ALEXANDER BOWIE was born on 26 Oct 1856 in Mercer County, Pennsylvania. He died on 24 Feb 1939 in LaSalle, Illinois. He married ELLEN DUNCAN. She was born in Dec 1863 in Scotland. She died on 13 May 1947 in LaSalle, Illinois.

25.   iii. ISABELLA BOWIE was born in Jun 1860 in Mercer County, Pennsylvania. She married (UNKNOWN). She married (2) WILLIAM STONE on 13 Oct 1891 in Mercer County, Pennsylvania. He was born in Jan 1857 in England. She married (UNKNOWN).

26.   iv. JOANNA BOWIE was born in Nov 1862 in Hickory Township, Mercer County, Pennsylvania. She died in 1945 in Mercer County, Pennsylvania. She married Robert Harris, son of John Harris and Isabella (unknown) on 20 May 1890 in Mercer County, Pennsylvania. He was born in Mar 1865 in Coolspring Township, Mercer County, Pennsylvania. He died in 1939 in Mercer County, Pennsylvania.

v.   JANET BOWIE was born about 1864 in Pennsylvania. She married (UNKNOWN) CASSIDY.

26.   vi. JOSEPH BOWIE was born on 22 Nov 1867 in Hickory Township, Mercer County, Pennsylvania. He married Florella Zimmerman, daughter of Daniel Zimmerman and Tressa C. (unknown) on 14 Jul 1894 in Mercer County, Pennsylvania. She was born on 03 May 1872 in Hickory Township, Mercer County, Pennsylvania. She died

in 1919 in Mercer County, Pennsylvania.

27.   vii. MARGARET BOWIE was born on 25 Dec 1870 in Hickory Township, Mercer County, Pennsylvania. She died on 20 Oct 1931 in Struthers, Mahoning County, Ohio. She married Edward M. Irwin on 11 Nov 1891 in Mercer County, Pennsylvania. He was born in Aug 1871 in Pennsylvania. He died in Mahoning County, Ohio.

28.   viii. ELLEN BOWIE was born on 17 Sep 1875 in Hickory Township, Mercer County, Pennsylvania. She married Charles Lytle, son of J. S. Lytle on 08 May 1895 in Mercer County, Pennsylvania. He was born on 15 Apr 1870 in Mercer County, Pennsylvania. He died in 1911.

11.   EUPHEMIA^3 BOWIE (Hunter^2, Robert^1) was born on 31 Jan 1814 in Loanhead, Midlothian, Scotland. She died on 30 Mar 1902 in Waratah, NSW, Australia. She married William Smith, son of Robert Smith and Mary Campbell on 03 Mar 1833 in Lasswade, Midlothian, Scotland. He was born on 04 Nov 1813 in Lasswade, Midlothian, Scotland. He died about 1851 in Lasswade, Midlothian, Scotland.

More About Euphemia Bowie:
Burial: 31 Mar 1902 in Presbyterian Cemetery, Wallsend, NSW, Australia

More About William Smith:
Occupation: Coal Bearer

William Smith and Euphemia Bowie had the following children:

29.   i. ROBERT^4 SMITH was born on 24 Mar 1834 in Lasswade, Midlothian, Scotland. He died on 02 Mar 1918 in West Wallsend, NSW, Australia. He married Margaret Kerr, daughter of William Kerr and Ann Hilson on 14 Apr 1865 in Cockpen Manse, Midlothian, Scotland. She was born about 1843 in Leith, Edinburgh, Scotland. She died on 30 Sep 1898 in Plattsburg, Wallsend, NSW, Australia.

30.   ii. HUNTER SMITH was born about 1837 in Loanhead, Midlothian, Scotland. He died on 04 Oct 1914 in Wallsend, NSW, Australia. He married Agnes Lawson on 31 Dec 1858 in Barley Know, Scotland. She was born about 1837 in Barleydeen, Edinburgh, Scotland. She died on 30 Sep 1916 in Wallsend, NSW, Australia.

      iii. ISABELLA SMITH was born about 1839 in Lasswade, Midlothian, Scotland. She died in Loanhead, Midlothian, Scotland.

      iv. JOHN SMITH was born about 1846 in Scotland. He died in Wallsend, NSW, Australia.

      v. MARY SMITH was born about 1850.

12.   ROBERT^3 BOWIE (Hunter^2, Robert^1) was born on 05 Mar 1827 in Lasswade, Midlothian, Scotland. He died on 27 Apr 1911. He married Mary Young, daughter of Thomas Young and Marion Neilson on 09 Sep 1848 in Lasswade, Midlothian, Scotland. She was born on 06 Feb 1830 in Hunterfield, Midlothian, Scotland. She died on 06 Nov 1902 in Hunterfield, Midlothian, Scotland.

More About Robert Bowie:
Burial: 29 Apr 1911
Occupation: Coal Miner

More About Mary Young:

Burial: November 8, 1902

Robert Bowie and Mary Young had the following children:

31.   i. JANE[4] BOWIE was born in 1849 in Cockpen, Midlothian, Scotland. She died on 16 Jan 1931 in Dalkeith, Midlothian, Scotland. She married (1) JAMES DANIEL MILLER, son of Robert Miller and Margaret McDonald on 31 Dec 1873 in Hunterfield, Midlothian, Scotland. He was born in 1851. He died on 21 May 1876 in Hunterfield, Midlothian, Scotland. She married (2) JAMES KILGOUR DINGWALL, son of Robert Dingwall and Elizabeth Kilgour on 20 Jul 1883 in Edinburgh, Scotland. He was born on 16 Apr 1843 in Strathmiglo, Perth, Scotland. He died on 04 Apr 1931 in Dalkeith, Midlothian, Scotland.

     ii.   HUNTER BOWIE was born in 1851 in Cockpen, Midlothian, Scotland. He died on 28 May 1908 in Lasswade, Midlothian, Scotland.

     More About Hunter Bowie:
Occupation: Coal Miner

32.   iii. THOMAS YOUNG BOWIE was born in 1853 in Cockpen, Midlothian, Scotland. He died on 31 Aug 1919. He married ELIZABETH SMITH. She was born in 1855. She died on 22 Feb 1934 in Dalkeith, Midlothian, Scotland.

33.   iv. MARION BOWIE was born on 16 Oct 1855 in Lasswade, Midlothian, Scotland. She died on 29 Jul 1936 in Bonnyrigg, Midlothian, Scotland. She married George Kerr Brown on 10 Jun 1881. He was born on 16 Aug 1855. He died on 29 Jun 1926 in Bonnyrigg, Midlothian, Scotland.

     v.   ROBERT BOWIE was born on 02 Jun 1857 in Lasswade, Midlothian, Scotland.

     vi. ISABELLA BOWIE was born on 30 Jun 1859 in Cockpen, Midlothian, Scotland. She died on 28 Nov 1922. She married Robert Noble on 08 Jun 1882. He was born in 1854. He died on 20 May 1902.

     More About Isabella Bowie:
Burial: 30 Nov 1922 in Dalkeith Cemetery, Dalkeith, Midlothian, Scotland

     vii. JAMES BOWIE was born on 05 Feb 1861 in Newbattle, Midlothian, Scotland. He died on 08 Aug 1900. He married ELIZABETH ROSS.

     More About James Bowie:
Burial: 10 Aug 1900 in Dalkeith Cemetery, Dalkeith, Midlothian, Scotland
Occupation: Coal Miner

     viii. ALEXANDER BOWIE was born on 06 Aug 1862 in Newbattle, Midlothian, Scotland. He died on 04 Jun 1929. He married Margaret Baillie Anderson on 29 Jan 1884. She was born in 1860. She died on 28 Mar 1945.

     More About Alexander Bowie:
Burial: 07 Jun 1929 in Dalkeith Cemetery, Dalkeith, Midlothian, Scotland
Occupation: Colliery Clerk
Occupation: Justice of the Peace

34.   ix. RICHARD BOWIE was born on 15 Dec 1863 in Newbattle, Midlothian, Scotland. He died on 22 Aug 1928. He married ISABELLA BENNETT. She was born in 1870. She died on 04 Mar 1967.

    x. DAVID BOWIE was born on 21 Nov 1865 in Newbattle, Midlothian, Scotland.

    xi. MARY ANN BOWIE was born on 29 Mar 1867 in Cockpen, Midlothian, Scotland. She died about 1950. She married ROBERT DINGWALL. He was born on 30 Mar 1867 in Dalkeith, Midlothian, Scotland. He died about 1935.

    xii. EUPHEMIA BOWIE was born on 27 Jan 1869 in Cockpen, Midlothian, Scotland. She married ARCHIBALD BROWN. She married JAMES MCLEOD.

35.   xiii. ELIZABETH YOUNG BOWIE was born in 1871 in Cockpen, Midlothian, Scotland. She died on 21 Nov 1916. She married David W. Haggert on 31 Mar 1892 in Stobhill, Scotland. He died on 02 May 1955.

13. **MARION AUCHETERLONIE^3 HISLOP** (Euphemia^2 Bowie, Robert^1 Bowie) was born on 28 Aug 1828 in Lasswade, Midlothian, Scotland. She married John Stewart on 31 Dec 1849 in Old Monkland, Lanarkshire, Scotland. He was born about 1826 in Sorby, Wigtonshire, Scotland.

John Stewart and Marion Aucheterlonie Hislop had the following children:

    i. MARY^4 STEWART was born in 1849 in Coatbridge, Lanarkshire, Scotland.

    ii. ALEXANDER STEWART was born in 1851 in Coatbridge, Lanarkshire, Scotland.

14. **ROBERT^3 BOWIE** (Euphemia^2, Robert^1) was born on 11 Nov 1821 in Lasswade, Midlothian, Scotland. He died on 16 Nov 1906 in Timaru, New Zealand. He married **ANNE COLVILLE**. She was born on 16 Oct 1820 in Shotts, Lanarkshire, Scotland. She died on 26 Aug 1899 in Timaru, New Zealand.

More About Robert Bowie:

Occupation: ; Coal Miner

Robert Bowie and Anne Colville had the following children:

    i. ROBERT^4 BOWIE was born in 1842 in New Monkland, Lanarkshire, scotland.

    ii. ELIZABETH BOWIE was born in 1844 in New Monkland, Lanarkshire, scotland.

    iii. JOHN BOWIE was born in 1845 in New Monkland, Lanarkshire, scotland.

    iv. ALEXANDER BOWIE was born in 1846 in New Monkland, Lanarkshire, scotland.

    v. JAMES BOWIE was born in 1849 in New Monkland, Lanarkshire, scotland.

37.   vi. HUNTER BOWIE was born in 1852 in Old Monkland, Lanarkshire, Scotland. He married Margaret Cameron, daughter of Alexander Cameron and Jean Adam on 21 Jul 1874 in Old Monkland, Lanarkshire, Scotland. She was born on 06 Jul 1851 in Old Monkland, Lanarkshire, Scotland.

    vii. THOMAS BOWIE was born in 1854 in Old Monkland, Lanarkshire, scotland.

viii.   J OSEPH B OWIE was born on 27 Apr 1857 in Old Monkland, Lanarkshire, Scotland.

ix.   E UPHEMIA B OWIE was born on 31 Jan 1859 in Old Monkland, Lanarkshire, scotland.

x.   D ANIEL B OWIE was born on 03 May 1862 in Old Monkland, Lanarkshire, scotland.

xi.   W ILLIAM A LLISON B OWIE was born on 16 Oct 1865 in Old Monkland, Lanarkshire, scotland.

Generation 4

15.   **C ATHERINE** [4] **B OWIE** (John[3], Alexander[2], Robert[1]) was born on 28 Feb 1846 in Newbattle, Midlothian, Scotland. She died on 18 Aug 1923 in Grove City, Pennsylvania. She married George W. Crawford, son of Robert Crawford and Lillias Notman on 12 Apr 1862 in Sharon, Pennsylvania. He was born in 1840 in Scotland. He died on 22 Aug 1922 in Grove City, Pennsylvania.

More About Catherine Bowie:
Burial: Woodland Cemetery, Grove City, Pennsylvania

Notes for Catherine Bowie:
Headstone spells her first name as Katherine.

More About George W. Crawford:
Burial: Woodland Cemetery, Grove City, Pennsylvania
Immigration: 1854 to Mercer County, Pennsylvania
Living In: 1920 Grove City, Mercer County, Pennsylvania
Occupation: 1870 in Hickory, Mercer County, Pennsylvania; Coal Miner
Occupation: 1880 in Hickory, Mercer County, Pennsylvania; Miner
Occupation: 1900 in Pine, Mercer County, Pennsylvania; Grocer

George W. Crawford and Catherine Bowie had the following children:

i.   K ATHERINE[5] C RAWFORD was born about 1863 in Pennsylvania.

ii.   M ILDRED C RAWFORD was born about 1867 in Pennsylvania.

iii.   R OBERT C RAWFORD was born about 1869 in Pennsylvania.

iv.   B ELLE A. C RAWFORD was born about 1872 in Pennsylvania.

v.   M ARGARET C RAWFORD was born about 1874 in Pennsylvania. She died in 1960.

vi.   G EORGIA C RAWFORD was born in Aug 1878 in Pennsylvania. She married (UNKNOWN) M EYER.

More About Georgia Crawford:
Burial: Woodland Cemetery, Grove City, Pennsylvania
Living In: 1920 Georgia is living with her parents in Grove City, Pennsylvania.

vii.   J ENNIE C RAWFORD was born in Jan 1882 in Ohio.

viii.   H ENRIETTA B. C RAWFORD was born in Feb 1885 in Pennsylvania. She married Oliver H. Firm about 1907. He was born about 1883 in Pennsylvania.

More About Henrietta B. Crawford:
Living In: 1920 Henrietta and her husband are living with her parents in Grove City, Pennsylvania

16.   ISABELLA[4] BOWIE (John[3], Alexander[2], Robert[1]) was born in 1851 in Newbattle, Midlothian, Scotland. She died on 09 Jan 1891 in Pennsylvania. She married ROBERT VEITCH. He was born on 20 Nov 1839 in Edinbrurgh, Midlothian, Scotland. He died in 1900.

More About Isabella Bowie:
Burial: Grace United Methodist Church Cemetery, Grove City, Pennsylvania

More About Robert Veitch:
Occupation: 1870 in Hickory, Mercer County, Pennsylvania; Coal Miner
Occupation: 1880 in Hickory, Mercer County, Pennsylvania; Miner
Occupation: 1900 in Washington, Butler County, Pennsylvania; Coal Miner

Robert Veitch and Isabella Bowie had the following children:

    i.   ANDREW[5] VEITCH was born in 1870 in Pennsylvania. He died in 1943. He married MAY JENKINS.

    ii.   KATIE VEITCH was born about 1872 in Pennsylvania.

    iii.   JOHN VEITCH was born about 1875 in Pennsylvania. He died in 1900.

    iv.   ARCHIBALD VEITCH was born about 1878 in Pennsylvania. He died on 27 Sep 1888.

        More About Archibald Veitch:
        Burial: Grace United Methodist Church Cemetery, Grove City, Pennsylvania

    v.   ELIZABETH VEITCH was born in Sep 1881 in Pennsylvania. She died in 1972.

17.   JANE[4] BOWIE (John[3], Alexander[2], Robert[1]) was born on 13 Jan 1853 in Sharon, Pennsylvania. She died on 26 Jun 1922 in Richland Grove, Mercer County,Illinois. She married William McNeil, son of John McNeil and Katherine Carr on 22 Dec 1871 in Sharon, Pennsylvania. He was born on 26 Mar 1844 in Tranent, East Lothian, Scotland. He died on 05 Mar 1918 in Griffin, Mercer County, Illinois.

More About Jane Bowie:
Burial: 28 Jun 1922 in Cable Community Cemetery, Cable, Illinois
Living In: 1920 Living with her son, George, in Richland Grove, Mercer County, Illinois.

Notes for Jane Bowie:
Obit: Jane Bowie McNeil, born Jan 11, 1853 in Sharon Pennsylvania, died June 26 1922 in New Windsor 69 years old, buried in Cable Cemetery. Spouse was William McNeil married 1872 in Sharon, PA (actually 1871). Parents John and Kate Bowie. Survivors eight children and 4 sisters.

More About William McNeil:
Burial: 07 Mar 1918 in Cable Community Cemetery, Cable, Illinois
Occupation: 1880 in Hickory, Mercer County, Pennsylvania; Miner
Occupation: 1900 in Richland Grove, Mercer County, Illinois; Farmer
Occupation: 1910 in Richland Grove, Mercer County, Illinois; Farmer

Notes for William McNeil:
Obituary for William: William McNeil born Mar 26 1844 in Scotland, died Mar 5, 1918 at Griffin, IL buried in Cable Cemetery. Came to Pennsylvania in 1870 and moved to Cable in 1884. Married Jane Bowie Dec 22 1871. Children were Mrs. Katie Holliday, John McNeil, Alexander McNeil, Thomas McNeil, William McNeil, Walter McNeil and George McNeil. He has one brother Thomas McNeil.

William McNeil and Jane Bowie had the following children:

    i.   KATHERINE[5] MCNEIL was born on 06 Dec 1872 in Jackson Center, Mercer county, Pennsylvania. She died on 10 Nov 1926 in Mercer County, Illinois. She married Clarence Jesse Holliday, son of James John Holliday and Charlotte Love on 16 Mar 1898. He was born on 22 Sep 1876 in Swedona, Mercer County, Illinois. He died on 12 Dec 1960 in Mercer County, Illinois.

    More About Katherine McNeil:
    Burial: Western Cemetery, Swedona, Mercer County, Illinois

    Notes for Katherine
    McNeil: Obit:
    Kate McNeil, only daughter of William and Jane McNeil was born at Jackson Center, Mercer County, Penn, December 6, 1872. She came with her parents and brothers to Cable in 1884 where she grew to womanhood

    She was married to Jess Holliday on March 16 1898. They lived for a time in Griffin, later moving to Sherrard and finally to the home where she passed away, November 10, 1926.

    "Aunt Kate" as she was affectionally called by many, was a devoted wife, a kind and loving mother, a true friend and neighbor, often going beyond her strength to aid someone. She was an unusually broad minded, kind and generous hearted lady, always looking for the good and doing all within her power. Every ready with a kind work and help where most needed. Mrs. Holliday was a firm believer in her Savior, always striving to follow the "Golden Rule."

    The only daughter, Mabel, passed from this life seven years ago. Since then Mrs. Holliday has not been well, though seldom complained, nor said much about her health but was over thoughtful of her dear ones.

    She leaves to mourn her going, the kind and faithful husband, one son, James, his wife and little girl, Janet of East Moline; five brothers, sisters-in-law; many nieces and nephews besides countless friends. Mrs Holliday had a large circle of friends and will be sadly missed by everyone. It is hard to understand just why she should be called so young, but this we know, God doeth all things well.

Funeral services were held at the home at 1:30 pm on Friday, Rev. C.E. Hoff of Sherrard officiating.

The following trio from Sherrard rendered several beautiful songs, Mrs. John E. Nelson, Mrs. Ben Kettering and Mrs. Victor Swanson.

The pall bearers were: John McNeil (her brother), George McNeil (her brother), Walter McNeil (her brother), Luther McNeil (her nephew, John's son), Tom McNeil (her brother) and Leslie Ralston (her nephew, Mary Arilla Holliday Ralston son). Internment took place in the Swedona Cemetery. (She shares a stone with her husband and daughter)

----

ii.   JOHN MCNEIL was born on 05 Oct 1875 in Sharon, Mercer County, Pennsylvania. He died on 18 Jul 1954 in Matherville, Mercer County, Illinois. He married Mathilda May Nimrick, daughter of Charles Thomas Nimrick and Rachel Tush on 27 Apr 1898. She was born in Oct 1876 in Cable, Mercer County, Illinois. She died in Mercer County, Illinois.

More About John McNeil:
Burial: Farlow Grove Cemetery, Matherville, Mercer County, Illinois

Notes for John McNeil:
MATHERVILLE, ILL- Funeral services for John McNeil, 79, resident of Matherville 45 years, will be held at 2 p.m. (CST) Wednesday at the Crummy Funeral Home in Viola. Burial will be in the Farlow Grove cemetery at Matherville. Mr. McNeil died Sunday afternoon in the Mercer county hospital. He had been in ill health a year. Mr. McNeil, was born Oct. 5, 1875 in Sharon, Pa. the family moving to Cable when he was nine years old. He had lived in the Cable, Sherrard and Matherville communities. The survivors, the widow, the former May Nimrick of Moline whom he married April 27, 1898; a son, Luther of Alpha; three brothers, Tom of Sherrard, Walter of East Moline and George of Galesburg; and a granddaughter.

----

iii.   ALEXANDER MCNEIL was born on 13 Jan 1878 in Sharon, Mercer County, Pennsylvania. He died on 23 Apr 1921 in Mercer County, Illinois. He married Clara Bell Holliday, daughter of James John Holliday and Charlotte Love on 21 Sep 1899. She was born on 28 Mar 1881 in New Windsor, Mercer County, Illinois. She died on 1   Oct 1954 in Mercer County, Illinois.

More About Alexander McNeil:
Burial: Western Cemetery, Swedona, Mercer County, Illinois
Cause Of Death: ; Kicked in the head by a horse.

Notes for Alexander McNeil:
obit: Alexander McNeil born Jan 13, 1878 in Sharon Pennsylvania, died Apr 23, 1921 in Richland Grove Township, buried in Swedona. Spouse Clara Bell Holliday married Sept 21, 1899. Parents William and Jane Bowie McNeil. He was kicked in

the head by a horse. Survivors: Mrs. Vesta Hubbard and Lottie; One sister
Kate Holliday; five brothers John, Thomas, William, Walter and George.

----

iv.   THOMAS MCNEIL was born on 12 Oct 1883 in Youngstown, Westmoreland County,
Pennsylvania. He died on 11 Nov 1957 in Elmwood, Illinois. He married Mary R.
Nimrick, daughter of Charles Nimrick and Wealthy Mead on 28 Dec 1910 in
Matherville, Illinois. She was born on 12 Jan 1887 in Griffin, Mercer County,
Illinois. She died on 23 Jan 1977 in Galesburg, Knox County, Illinois.

More About Thomas McNeil:
Burial: Cable community Cemetery, Cable, Mercer County, Illinois

Notes for Thomas McNeil:
Aledo Democrat 13 Nov 1957 Obit:
Thomas McNeil born Oct 12, 1883 in Youngstown, PA , he died November 11,
1957 in Elmwood, IL. His burial is in Cable Cemtery, Parents William and Jane
Boyne (Bowie) McNeil. Came to Cable in infancy. He married Mary R. Nimrick
on December 28, 1910. They had three children: Ralph, Richard and Mrs.
Leslie C. Snyder. He has a brother George.

----

v.   WILLIAM MCNEIL was born on 06 Aug 1886 in Cable, Mercer County, Illinois. He
died on 13 Feb 1934 in Galesburg, Knox County, Illinois. He married Esther
Rosene, daughter of Peter Rosene and Amanda Sophia Carlson on 30 Dec 1908
in Aledo, Illinois. She was born on 17 Jul 1888 in Cable, Mercer County, Illinois.
She died on 23 Sep 1981 in Akron, Summit County, Ohio.

More About William McNeil:
Burial: New Windsor Cemetery,New Windsor, Mercer County,
Illinois

Cause Of Death: Burns received in a house fire.

Notes for William McNeil:
Aledo Democrat, Feb 21, 1934 Obit William McNeil was born August 6, 1886 near
New Windsor and died February 13, 1934 in Galesburg from burns received while
trying to rescue his daughter Ruby in a house fire, she was already safe. Williams
parents were William and Jane Bowie McNeil. William married Esther Rosene
August 1909. They had three daughters Evelyn of Cambridge, Ruby and
Genevieve at home. William had four brothers George of Galesburg, Thomas of
Sherrard, James of East Moline and Walter of New Windsor. Burial will be in New
Windsor Cemetery.

----

vi.   WALTER MCNEIL was born on 02 Jan 1888 in New Windsor, Mercer County, Illinois. He
died on 26 Sep 1954 in Mercer County, Illinois. He married Hilda A. Tornquist,
daughter of Ludwig A. Tornquist and Matilda G. (unknown) on 04 Mar 1909 in Aledo,
Mercer County, Illinois. She was born on 01 Aug 1880 in Mercer County,

Illinois. She died on 10 Jan 1953 in Rock Island County, Illinois.

More About Walter McNeil:
Burial: New Windsor Cemetery, New Windsor, Mercer County, Illinois

Notes for Walter McNeil:
28 Sept 1954, pg.19 , Galesburg-Register Mail
NEW WINDSOR- Walter McNeil, 66, of Moline, a former New Windsor resident, died Sunday at 1 a.m. at the home of his son-in-law and daughter, Mr. and Mrs. Wallace Flack, Rio, where he was spending the weekend. He was born Jan. 2, 1888 at New Windsor and was married to Hilda Tornquist of New Windsor March 25, 1900, at Aledo. They lived on farms in the New Windsor and Orion communities until 1948 when they went to Moline. He was employed by the John Deere Co. in Moline. Mrs. McNeil died in 1953. Survivors are two sons, Eugene of Orion and Vernon of New Windsor; three daughters, Mrs. Robert Trunmel of East Moline, Mrs. Edward Nicholson of Moline and Mrs. Flack; two brothers, Tom of Cable and George of Galesburg; 14 grandchildren and two great-grandchildren. A sister and three brothers also preceded him in death. Funeral services will be conducted Tuesday at 2 p.m. at the New Windsor Presbyterian Church by the Rev. Henry Stamm of Rio. Burial will be in the New Windsor Cemetery. Friends may call from 7 to 9 o'clock this evening at the Knox-Wallin Funeral home in Alpha and Tuesday after 10 a.m. at the church.

----

vii.   GEORGE WASHINGTON MCNEIL was born on 22 Feb 1891 in New Windsor, Mercer County, Illinois. He died on 05 Aug 1966 in Galesburg, Knox County, Illinois. He married Melvina Jane Ralston, daughter of Ralph Ralston and Alice Wilson on 26 May 1920 in Rock Island, Illinois. She was born on 29 Mar 1900 in New Windsor, Mercer County, Illinois. She died on 28 Dec 1987 in Galesburg, Knox County, Illinois.

More About George Washington McNeil:
Burial: East Linwood Cemetery, Galesburg, Knox County, Illinois
Occupation: Galesburg, Illinois; Automobile Mechanic

Notes for George Washington McNeil:
Obituary: Galesburg Register-Mail, Saturday, Aug 6, 1966

George W. "Tuck" McNeil, 75, of Galesburg route 2 died Friday at 2:20 p.m. at St. Mary's Hospital. Mr McNeil had been an automobile mechanic here for 40 years, retiring 1962.

He was born Feb 22, 1891 at New Windsor. He married Melvina J. Ralston at Rock Island May 26, 1920. She survives with three sons, Robert D. with the Air Force at Chanute Field, Goerge Jr. of Galesburg and Wayne L. of Abingdon; three daughters, Mrs. Vivian Ryan of New Windsor, Mrs. Mabel Sholl of Clarence, MO, Mrs. Alice LaJune Stanton of Knoxville and Mrs. Lillian Arghast of Galesburg; 23 grandchildren and six great-grandchildren.

Funeral will be Tuesday at 2 p.m. at Kimber and West Chapel, where friends may call Monday evening. Burial will be at East Linwood Cemetery.

----

    viii.   JAMES ARTHUR MCNEIL was born on 11 Apr 1893 in New Windsor, Mercer County, Illinois. He died on 09 Sep 1949 in East Moline, Rock Island County, Illinois,. He married Elsie Russ, daughter of George Russ and Mary Heine on 28 Jun 1921 in Rock Island County, Illinois. She was born on 20 Aug 1898 in Rock Island, Rock Island County, Illinois. She died on 15 Mar 1956 in Rock Island County, Illinois.

More About James Arthur McNeil:
Burial: Chippiannock Cemetery, Rock Island, Rock Island County, Illinois
Military Service: World War One

Notes for James Arthur McNeil:
Obit: Moline Paper, Sept 10, 1949
James M'Neil, 56, is Victim of Heart Attack-Formerly operated lunchroom;Funeral services will be held Saturday.

 James A. McNeil, 56, 251 Sixteenth Avenue, East Moline, died suddenly following a heart attack in his home about 7:15 o'clock last night before a physician arrived. Fireman rushed the city's respirator to the McNeil home, but attempts to revive him were futile.
 Mr. McNeil, a resident of East Moline for the last 32 years, formerly operated a combined lunch room and billiard parlor. He sold his business about 8 years ago and since then had been employed as a machinist at the American Machine and Metals, Inc.
 He was born in Cable, April 11, 1893, the son of Jess and Kate McNeil. He married Elsie Russ, niece of the late F.C. Heine, in Rock Island on June 21, 1921. He served as a corporal overseas in the First World War.
 Survivors besides the Widow and a daughter, Jane Bracke of Moline and a son Donald McNeil at home and a grandchild.
 The body was removed to VanHoe funeral home where services will be held at 2 o'clock Saturday afternoon. The Rev. Fred J. Rolf, pastor of the Church of Peace in Rock Island, will be officiating. Burial will be in Chippiannock Cemetery, Rock Island.

Head Stone has 1892 for year of birth. World War Two draft registration gives April 11, 1893 as date of birth.

18.   MARGARET[4] BOWIE (John[3], Alexander[2], Robert[1]) was born on 25 Apr 1856 in Massilon, Stark County, Ohio. She died on 06 Aug 1943 in Krebs, Oklahoma. She married (1) DAVID ARCHIBALD about 1877. He was born in 1845 in Scotland. He died in May 1882 in Krebs, Indian Territory (Present Day Oklahoma). She married (2) PHILIP KEWLEY about 1890. He was born on 17 Jul 1846 in England. He died on 30 Nov 1931 in Pittsburg County, Oklahoma.

More About Margaret Bowie:
Burial: Oak Hill Memorial Park, McAlester, Oklahoma
Living In: 15 Jun 1880 Margaret and her children, Thomas and Katherine, are living with Margaret's mother in Hickory, Pennsylvania.
Living In: 1940 Krebs, Pittsburg County, Oklahoma

Notes for Margaret Bowie:
1900 U.S. Census has July 1858 as birth date.

Another Krebs pioneer, Mrs. Margaret Kewley, who had resided there since 1880, passed away Friday evening at her home. She has been failing in heath for some time. She was born in Massilion, Ohio, April 25, 1856 and moved to Pennsylvania with her parents. On January 1, 1877 she married David Archibald who met death in a cyclone that swept the Krebs area in May 1882. In 1887 Mrs. Archibald remarried, being united with Phillip Kewley, who passed away in 1931. She had been a member of the Krebs Rebekah Lodge since 1886. Four sons, Tom Archibald, Dave Archibald, Alex Kewley and Phil Kewley, all of Krebs, survive. She also leaves a sister, Mrs. Ellen Lewis of Grove City, Pa. Five grandchildren and a great grandson mourn her passing. Funeral services are to be conducted at 2:30 p.m. Sunday, at the late home, with Dr. Lawrence Johnson, of the First Presbyterian Church officiating. The pallbearers will be Rass Martin, John Holstead, Tom Otterson, Bill Collins, Dick Dixon, Rock Fernell. Chaney's will be in charge of interment
----

Krebs Rebekas Hold Memorial for Mrs. Kewley

A memorial service for the only member of Krebs Rebekah Lodge number 2 to have passed away during the year, was held Wednesday night in Krebs. The lovely candlelight ceremony was for Mrs. Margaret Kewley, and members taking part were Annie Watson, noble grand; Bertha Gilpin, vice grans; Tenie Klink, warden; Mary Romano, conductor; Tressa Poletto, crepe bearer; Beulah Bailey, flower bearer; Mary Jane Redpath, chaplain; Henrietta Teagarde, Esther Eustis, Minnie Martin and Alpha Oxford, S.D.P. The Rebekah president, Mrs. Beulah B. Davidson of Tulsa, and Mrs. Nita Maytubby of Wewoka, vice president, were special guests of the lodge, and other visitors from McAlester and Wewoka were in attendance.
(McAlester News-Captal, July 1, 1944)

More About David Archibald:
Burial: North McAlester Cemetery, McAlester, Oklahoma

David Archibald and Margaret Bowie had the following children:

      i.   THOMAS[5] ARCHIBALD was born on 25 Dec 1878 in Hermitage, Pennsylvania. He died on 29 Oct 1965 in Pittsburg County, Oklahoma.

          More About Thomas Archibald:
          Burial: Oak Hill Memorial Park, McAlester, Oklahoma
          Living In: 1900 Living with his mother and stepfather in Township 5, Choctaw Nation, Indian Territory. (present day Oklahoma)
          Living In: 1910 Living with his mother and step father in Krebs, Oklahoma
          Living In: 1920 Living with his mother and step father in Krebs, Oklahoma
          Living In: 1930 Living with his mother and step father in Krebs, Oklahoma
          Living In: 1940 Living with his mother in Krebs, Oklahoma
          Occupation: 1910 in Krebs, Pittsburg County, Oklahoma; Coal Miner
          Occupation: 1918; Coal Miner, Osage Coal Company, Krebs, Oklahoma
          Occupation: 1920 in Krebs, Pittsburg County, Oklahoma; Coal Miner
          Occupation: 1930 in Alderson, Pittsburg County, Oklahoma; Coal Miner

          Notes for Thomas Archibald:
          Head Stone has December 25, 1878 as date of birth.
          World War One draft registration has September 17, 1877 as date of birth.

1900 U.S. census has January 1878 as date of birth.

    ii.   KATHERINE ARCHIBALD was born on 19 Feb 1880 in Pennsylvania. She died on 06 Nov 1928 in Krebs, Oklahoma. She married (1) EDWARD SMITH on 09 Jul 1900 in Krebs, Indian Territory (Present Day Oklahoma). He was born about 1879. She married JAMES WATSON. He was born on 07 Dec 1882. He died on 12 Oct 1971.

        More About Katherine Archibald:
        Burial: Oak Hill Memorial Park, McAlester, Oklahoma
        Living In: 1900 Choctaw Nation, Indian Territory

    iii.   DAVID ARCHIBALD was born on 17 Jan 1883 in Hermitage, Pennsylvania. He died on 18 Jan 1975 in Pittsburg County, Oklahoma.

        More About David Archibald:
        Burial: Oak Hill Memorial Park, McAlester, Oklahoma
        Living In: 1910 Living with his mother and stepfather in Krebs, Oklahoma
        Living In: 1920 Living with his mother and step father in Krebs, Oklahoma
        Living In: 1940 Living with his mother in Krebs, Oklahoma.
        Occupation: 1910 in Krebs, Pittsburg County, Oklahoma; Coal Miner
        Occupation: 1918 in Krebs, Oklahoma; Coal Miner, Osage Coal Company
        Occupation: 1920 in Krebs, Pittsburg County, Oklahoma; Coal Miner
        Occupation: 1940 in Krebs, Pittsburg County, Oklahoma; Coal Mine Electrician

        Notes for David Archibald:
        Headstone has date of birth as January 17, 1882. Social Security death index has date of birth as January 17, 1883. 1900 U.S. Census has date of birth as January 1883.

More About Philip Kewley:
Burial: Oak Hill Memorial Park, McAlester, Oklahoma
Immigration: 1867 Emigrated from England.
Occupation: 1900 in Township 5, Choctaw Nation, Indian Territory (present day Oklahoma); Coal Miner
Occupation: 1910 in Krebs, Pittsburg County, Oklahoma; Restaurant Proprietor
Occupation: 1920 in Krebs, Pittsburg County, Oklahoma; Retired
Occupation: 1930 in Alderson, Pittsburg County, Oklahoma; Retired

Notes for Philip Kewley:
1900 U.S. Census has July 1850 as birth date.

Philip Kewley and Margaret Bowie had the following children:

    i.   ALEXANDER[5] KEWLEY was born on 17 Jul 1891 in Indian Territory (Present Day Oklahoma). He died on 20 Mar 1977 in Pittsburg County, Oklahoma.

        More About Alexander Kewley:
        Burial: Oak Hill Memorial Park, McAlester, Oklahoma
        Living In: 1920 Living with his parents in Krebs, Oklahoma
        Living In: 1930 Living with his parents in Alderson, Pittsburg county, Oklahoma
        Living In: 1940 Living with his mother in Krebs, oklahoma
        Occupation: 1910 in Krebs, Pittsburg County, Oklahoma; Coal Miner

Occupation: 1920 in Krebs, Pittsburg County, Oklahoma; Coal Miner
Occupation: 1930 in Alderson, Pittsburg County, Oklahoma; Pool Hall Operator
Occupation: 1940 in Krebs, Pittsburg County, Oklahoma; Coal Mine Loader

    ii.   PHILIP KEWLEY was born on 21 May 1897 in Indian Territory (Present Day Oklahoma). He died on 27 Feb 1960 in McAlester, Pittsburg County, Oklahoma.

More About Philip Kewley:
Burial: Oak Hill Memorial Park, McAlester, Oklahoma
Living In: 1920 Living with his parents in Krebs, Oklahoma
Living In: 1940 Living with his mother in Krebs, oklahoma
Occupation: 1910 in Krebs, Pittsburg County, Oklahoma; Coal Mine Driver
Occupation: 1920 in Krebs, Pittsburg County, Oklahoma; Coal Miner
Occupation: 1940 in Krebs, Pittsburg County, Oklahoma; Coal Mine Loader
Military Service: U.S. Navy, World War One

Notes for Philip Kewley:
1900 U.S. census has birth date as May 1896.

19.   **ALEXANDER[4] BOWIE** (John[3], Alexander[2], Robert[1]) was born about 22 Dec 1858 in Pennsylvania. He died on 04 Mar 1889 in McAlester, Indian Territory (Present Day Oklahoma). He married **BARBARA PATTERSON BELL**. She was born on 03 Mar 1867 in Silverbanks, Cambuslang, Lanarkshire, Scotland. She died on 12 Mar 1936 in Oklahoma City, Oklahoma.

More About Alexander Bowie:
Burial: North McAlester Cemetery, McAlester, Oklahoma

More About Barbara Patterson Bell:
Burial: 15 Mar 1936 in Coalgate Cemetery, Coalgate, Oklahoma
Immigration: 22 Jul 1871 Arrived in New York, New York on ship "India"

Notes for Barbara Patterson Bell:
Headstone has February 24, 1868 for date of birth.

Alexander Bowie and Barbara Patterson Bell had the following child:

    i.   ANNIE BELL[5] BOWIE was born on 11 Mar 1886 in Krebs, Indian Territory (Present Day Oklahoma). She died on 31 Jan 1978 in Amarillo, Potter County, Texas. She married Claude Ray Badgett, son of James Royal Badgett and Mary Belle Wakefield on 16 Apr 1902 in Coalgate, Choctaw Nation, Indian Territory (Present Day Oklahoma). He was born on 27 Jan 1881 in Kentuckytown, Grayson County, Texas. He died on 18 Apr 1960 in Plainview, Texas.

More About Annie Bell Bowie:
Burial: Rest Haven Cemetery, Quitaque, Texas

Notes for Annie Bell Bowie:
Listed in Choctaw Nations Marriage records (Oklahoma).
----
lived in Silverton, Texas at the time of her death.

Headstone has January 30, 1978 for date of death. Death certificate has January 31, 1978 for date of death.

----

20.   **ELLEN**[4] **BOWIE** (John[3], Alexander[2], Robert[1]) was born in Apr 1861 in Mercer County, Pennsylvania. She died after 01 May 1940. She married John Lewis about 1882. He was born in Aug 1860 in England. He died between 16 Jan 1920-10 Apr 1930.

More About Ellen Bowie:
Living In: 1930 Living with her son, Homer, and his family in Meadville, Crawford County, Pennsylvania
Living In: 1940 Living with her daughter, Ellen, in Grove City, Mercer County, Pennsylvania.

More About John Lewis:
Occupation: 1900 in Parsons, Labette County, Kansas; Butcher
Occupation: 1910 in Keytesville, Chariton County, Missouri; Butcher in Butcher shop
Occupation: 1920 in Hickory, Mercer County, Pennsylvania; Meat Market Butcher

John Lewis and Ellen Bowie had the following children:

   i.   HOMER NELSON[5] LEWIS was born on 21 Apr 1891 in Fleming, Missouri. He married VERDA S. (UNKNOWN).

   More About Homer Nelson Lewis:
   Occupation: 1930 in Meadville, Crawford County, Pennsylvania; Clerk in Steam Rail Road Office
   Occupation: 1942 in Meadville, Pennsylvania; Working for Erie Railroad Company

   ii.   RAYMOND JOHN LEWIS was born on 14 Aug 1896 in Orrick, Missouri.

   More About Raymond John Lewis:
   Occupation: 1942 in Fort Wayne, Indiana; Working for Nickel Plate Rail Road

   iii.   ELLA MARY LEWIS was born in May 1899 in Kansas. She died in Jun 1964.

   More About Ella Mary Lewis:
   Living In: 1930 Living with her brother, Homer, in Meadville, Crawford County, Pennsylvania.
   Occupation: 1940 in Grove City, Mercer County, Pennsylvania; Working for W.P.A.

21.   **EUPHEMIA**[4] **BOWIE** (John[3], Alexander[2], Robert[1]) was born on 25 Mar 1864 in Pennsylvania. She died on 02 May 1936 in Krebs, Pittsburg County, Oklahoma. She married John Evans, son of James Evans and Anna Harrison about 1880 in Hickory Township, Mercer County, Pennsylvania. He was born on 14 Sep 1859 in Pennsylvania. He died on 09 Mar 1942 in Pittsburg County, Oklahoma.

More About Euphemia Bowie:
Burial: Oak Hill Memorial Park, McAlester, Oklahoma

More About John Evans:
Burial: Oak Hill Memorial Park, McAlester, Oklahoma
Occupation: 1900 in Township 5, Choctaw Nation, Indian Territory (present day Oklahoma); Miner

Occupation: 1910 in Krebs, Pittsburg County, Oklahoma; Coal Miner
Occupation: 1920 in Krebs, Pittsburg County, Oklahoma; Coal Miner
Occupation: 1930 in Alderson, Pittsburg County, Oklahoma; Retired
Occupation: 1940 in Krebs, Pittsburg County, Oklahoma; Retired

John Evans and Euphemia Bowie had the following children:

    i.   JOHN[5] EVANS was born on 27 Dec 1883 in Pennsylvania. He died in Nov 1976.

    ii.   JAMES EVANS was born in Jun 1885 in Ohio.

        More About James Evans:
        Living In: 1910 Living wih his parents in Krebs, Oklahoma
        Occupation: 1910 in Krebs, Pittsburg County, Oklahoma; Coal Miner

    iii.   ANNIE EVANS was born in Mar 1890 in Indian Territory (Oklahoma).

        More About Annie Evans:
        Living In: Bet. 1910-1930 Living wiith her parents in Pittsburg County, Oklahoma
        Living In: 1940 Living with her father in Krebs, Oklahoma
        Occupation: 1920 in Krebs, Pittsburg County, Oklahoma; Sales Lady in Dry Goods Store
        Occupation: 1930 in Alderson, Pittsburg County, Oklahoma; Sales Lady in Dry Goods Store

    iv.   IRENE EVANS was born on 14 Nov 1897 in Krebs, Indian Territory (Oklahoma). She died on 21 Jan 1969 in Dallas, Dallas County, Texas. She married (UNKNOWN) WILCOX.

        More About Irene Evans:
        Burial: Memorial Park Cemetery, Tulsa, Oklahoma
        Occupation: 1969; Clothing Sales Lady

    v.   ALEXANDER BOWIE EVANS was born on 09 Oct 1902. He died in Nov 1978.

        More About Alexander Bowie Evans:
        Occupation: 1920 in Krebs, Pittsburg County, Oklahoma; Coal Miner

    vi.   MARGARET EVANS was born about 1906.

    vii.   EUPHEMIA EVANS was born about Nov 1909.

        More About Euphemia Evans:
        Occupation: 1930 in Alderson, Pittsburg County, Oklahoma; Stenographer in Law Office

22.   **JAMES[4] LAING** (Margaret[3] Bowie, Alexander[2] Bowie, Robert[1] Bowie) was born on 02 Jan 1846 in Airdrie, Lanark, Scotland. He died on 31 Oct 1907 in Lewisburg, West Virginia. He married Susanna Kay, daughter of Thomas Kay and Janet Kerr on 31 Dec 1872. She was born on 29 Apr 1851 in Lanark, Scotland. She died on 30 Apr 1937 in Lewisburg, West Virginia.

More About James Laing:
Burial: Old Stone Prebyterian Church Cemetery, Lewisburg, West Virginia
Immigration: 1867 to United States
Living In: 1870 Living with his parents in Hickory, Mercer County, Pennsylvania.
Occupation: 1870 in Hickory, Mercer County, Pennsylvania; Coal Miner

Notes for James Laing:
    History of Greenbrier County, by J. R. Cole, Lewisburg, WV 1917 p. 130-132   JAMES
LAING 1846-1907
James Laing, son of John and Margaret Bowie Laing, was born at Slamanan, near the city of
Glasgow, Scotland, January 2, 1846.
    Mr. Laing's parents, realizing the larger possibilities that the United States offered,
emigrated with their family to America in 1866, settling in Mercer county, Pennsylvania, where
they engaged in farming and mining. On December 31, 1872, Mr. Laing was married to
Susanna Kay, second daughter of Thomas and Janet Kerr Kay. Miss Kay was a Scotch lady,
born at Lanark, Scotland, April 29, 1851, and came to America with her parents in 1870. The
Kay family settled first in Sharon, Pa., and later in West Virginia.
    Mr. Laing bought a large tract of coal land in West Virginia and moved with his family of two
children to Quinnimont, Fayette County, in 1878. At this time the New River coal fields were just
beginning to be developed. Mr. Laing organized the Royal Coal and Coke Company in 1891
and opened up the Royal mine, which was the first mine to be operated in Raleigh county, and
was managed by Mr. Laing until 1896, when he organized the Sun Coal and Coke Company
and sank the first shaft ever used in the New River coal field, at Sun, which he managed with
remarkable effectiveness and success. Mr. Laing continued the management of these mines
until 1904, when he retired from active service in mining operations, though he continued his
interest in other activities, and until the time of his death was president of the Laing Mining
Company, the McKinley Land Company, the Craig-Giles Iron Company and the Mountain Lake
Land Company.
    Mr. Laing had long dreamed of spending his declining years in a quiet country community,
and selecting the small but well-known town of Lewisburg, purchased property and built a large
and handsome stone house, "Canipsie Glen," into which he moved his family from Fayette
county, in 1904.Mr. Laing was a trustee of the Lewisburg Seminary, from which institution his
daughters received their education. This school was dear to his heart and he labored zealously
for its development and power. His interest in Christian education was felt over the entire church,
and in 1907, shortly before his death, he was appointed a trustee of Hampden-Sidney College,
where two of his sons had been educated.
    He was just realizing the ambition of his boyhood comfort and quietness for himself and his
loyal and saintly wife and having a constructive part in the education of the youth of his beloved
State and church-when his death occurred, after a brief illness, at his home in Lewisburg, October
31, 1907. Surviving him are his widow and seven children: Janet Kerr, John Bowie, Thomas Kay,
Annie Jean, James Kay, Susanna Kay (Mrs. R. L. Speas), and Bessie Belle.
    Like most of his Scotch countrymen, Mr. Laing was an ardent Presbyterian, devoted to his
church and liberal in its support. While at Quinnimont, in 1882, he was ordained a ruling elder
in the church, and with a fidelity and fitness realized by few, he served in that sacred capacity
wherever he lived.
    Mr. Laing lived in Lewisburg only three short years, but it was long enough to win an enviable
place in the esteem and friendship of the people of the town and community. In politics, he was
a Republican, believing firmly in the McKinley principles of protection. As a man and citizen his
life and conduct were ever above reproach, modest and unassuming, true to his convictions and
firm in his stand for right as he saw it; he held the respect and confidence of those who knew
him best and was admired and honored by his many business associates and employees. In his
death his family lost one of the truest and best husbands and fathers, the schools of which he
was a trustee a wise and trusted counselor, his town and State a constructive and loyal citizen,
and the church, his choicest pride, a most faithful member and officer.

More About Susanna Kay:
Burial: Old Stone Prebyterian Church Cemetery, Lewisburg, West Virginia
Immigration: 1870 to Sharon, Pennsylvania

James Laing and Susanna Kay had the following children:

     i.   JOHN BOWIE[5] LAING was born on 23 Sep 1876 in Mercer County, Pennsylvania. He died on 15 Feb 1946. He married Margaret Nelson on 20 Apr 1898.

    ii.   JANET KERR LAING.

    iii.   THOMAS KAY LAING.

    iv.   ANNIE JEAN LAING.

    v.   JAMES KAY LAING.

    vi.   SUSANNA KAY LAING. She married R. L. SPEAS.

    vii.   BESSIE BELLE LAING. She married CHARLES M. MCWHORTER.

    viii.   MARGARET LAING.

Notes for Margaret Laing: Died in Infancy.

23.   **ALEXANDER[4] BOWIE** (Hunter[3], Alexander[2], Robert[1]) was born on 26 Oct 1856 in Mercer County, Pennsylvania. He died on 24 Feb 1939 in LaSalle, Illinois. He married **ELLEN DUNCAN**. She was born in Dec 1863 in Scotland. She died on 13 May 1947 in LaSalle, Illinois.

More About Alexander Bowie:
Burial: 28 Feb 1939 in Oakwood Cemetery, LaSalle, Illinois
Living In: 1900 LaSalle, Illinois
Occupation: 1880; Miner
Occupation: 1900; Carpenter

Notes for Alexander Bowie:
1900 U.S. Census gives Alexander's birth date as October 1857. Death record gives his birth date as October 26, 1856.

More About Ellen Duncan:
Burial: 15 May 1947 in Oak Wood Cemetery, LaSalle, Illinois

Alexander Bowie and Ellen Duncan had the following child:

    i.   HUNTER[5] BOWIE was born on 06 Jan 1887 in LaSalle, Illinois. He died on 25 Mar 1943 in LaSalle, Illinois. He married WINIFRED DUFFY.

        More About Hunter Bowie:
        Burial: 27 Mar 1943 in Forest Park Cemetery, LaSalle, Illinois
        Occupation: Carpenter

24.   ISABELLA[4] BOWIE (Hunter[3], Alexander[2], Robert[1]) was born in Jun 1860 in Mercer County, Pennsylvania. She married (UNKNOWN). She married (2) WILLIAM STONE on 13 Oct 1891 in Mercer County, Pennsylvania. He was born in Jan 1857 in England. She married (UNKNOWN).

(Unknown) and Isabella Bowie had the following child:

      i.   JAMES ELMER[5] BOWIE was born on 08 Dec 1888 in Pennsylvania. He died on 09 Nov 1949 in Tucson, Arizona. He married Anna Powell in 1908. She was born on 12 Mar 1887 in Bethel, Pennsylvania. She died on 12 Nov 1944 in Marana, Arizona.

          More About James Elmer Bowie:
          Burial: 11 Nov 1949 in Tucson, Arizona

William Stone and Isabella Bowie had the following child:

      i.   EDWARD[5] STONE was born in Sep 1892 in Ohio.

(Unknown) and Isabella Bowie had the following child:

      i.   ANNIE[5] BOWIE. She married (UNKNOWN) FISHER.

25.   JOANNA[4] BOWIE (Hunter[3], Alexander[2], Robert[1]) was born in Nov 1862 in Hickory Township, Mercer County, Pennsylvania. She died in 1945 in Mercer County, Pennsylvania. She married Robert Harris, son of John Harris and Isabella (unknown) on 20 May 1890 in Mercer County, Pennsylvania. He was born in Mar 1865 in Coolspring Township, Mercer County, Pennsylvania. He died in 1939 in Mercer County, Pennsylvania.

Robert Harris and Joanna Bowie had the following children:

      i.   ELIZABETH[5] HARRIS was born in Aug 1891 in Mercer County, Pennsylvania.

      ii.   MARGARET HARRIS was born in Jun 1893 in Mercer County, Pennsylvania.

      iii.   ROBERT IRA HARRIS was born on 17 Sep 1895 in Mercer County, Pennsylvania.

      iv.   HOMER ADDISON HARRIS was born on 16 Sep 1899 in Mercer County, Pennsylvania.

      v.   MYRTLE HARRIS was born about 1902 in Mercer County, Pennsylvania.

      vi.   LAURA J. HARRIS was born about 1904 in Mercer County, Pennsylvania.

      vii.   VIOLA M. HARRIS was born about 1908 in Mercer County, Pennsylvania.

26.   JOSEPH[4] BOWIE (Hunter[3], Alexander[2], Robert[1]) was born on 22 Nov 1867 in Hickory Township, Mercer County, Pennsylvania. He married Florella Zimmerman, daughter of Daniel Zimmerman and Tressa C. (unknown) on 14 Jul 1894 in Mercer County, Pennsylvania. She was born on 03 May 1872 in Hickory Township, Mercer County, Pennsylvania. She died in 1919 in Mercer County, Pennsylvania.

Joseph Bowie and Florella Zimmerman had the following children:

      i.   TERRESA[5] BOWIE was born in May 1895 in Pennsylvania. She married Charley R. Billig on 04 Apr 1914 in Mercer County, Pennsylvania. He was born on 22 Nov 1895 in Pennsylvania.

      ii.   ALEXANDER BOWIE was born in May 1898 in Mercer County, Pennsylvania.

     iii.   JOSEPH BOWIE was born on 16 Jun 1905 in Mercer County, Pennsylvania. He died in Oct 1970 in Mercer County, Pennsylvania. He married FLORENCE M. (UNKNOWN). She was born on 09 Jan 1903. She died in Jan 1979 in Mercer County, Pennsylvania.

     iv.   EMMA BOWIE was born about 1909 in Mercer County, Pennsylvania.

     v.   WILLIAM BOWIE was born about 1911 in Mercer County, Pennsylvania.

27.   **MARGARET**[4] **BOWIE** (Hunter[3], Alexander[2], Robert[1]) was born on 25 Dec 1870 in Hickory Township, Mercer County, Pennsylvania. She died on 20 Oct 1931 in Struthers, Mahoning County, Ohio. She married Edward M. Irwin on 11 Nov 1891 in Mercer County, Pennsylvania. He was born in Aug 1871 in Pennsylvania. He died in Mahoning County, Ohio.

Edward M. Irwin and Margaret Bowie had the following children:

     i.   CLARENCE E.[5] IRWIN was born on 29 Aug 1892 in Pennsylvania. He died in Oct 1968 in Struthers, Ohio.

     ii.   OLIVER ROY IRWIN was born in Aug 1894 in Pennsylvania.

     iii.   NINA M. IRWIN was born on 24 May 1899 in Pennsylvania. She died on 27 Mar 1990 in Struthers, Ohio. She married William Hoffman about 1916 in Mahoning County, Ohio. He was born on 03 Apr 1895 in Ohio. He died in Aug 1972 in Struthers, Ohio.

28.   **ELLEN**[4] **BOWIE** (Hunter[3], Alexander[2], Robert[1]) was born on 17 Sep 1875 in Hickory Township, Mercer County, Pennsylvania. She married Charles Lytle, son of J. S. Lytle on 08 May 1895 in Mercer County, Pennsylvania. He was born on 15 Apr 1870 in Mercer County, Pennsylvania. He died in 1911.

Charles Lytle and Ellen Bowie had the following child:

     i.   GENEVA HELEN[5] LYTLE was born on 23 Sep 1896 in Sharpsville, Pennsylvania. She died on 22 Oct 1984 in Homeland, Riverside county, California. She married Harry Abram Flenner on 07 Jun 1952 in Yuma, Arizona. He was born on 27 Feb 1895 in San Diego, California. He died on 16 May 1977 in Loma Linda, California.

29.   **ROBERT**[4] **SMITH** (Euphemia[3] Bowie, Hunter[2] Bowie, Robert[1] Bowie) was born on 24 Mar 1834 in Lasswade, Midlothian, Scotland. He died on 02 Mar 1918 in West Wallsend, NSW, Australia. He married Margaret Kerr, daughter of William Kerr and Ann Hilson on 14 Apr 1865 in Cockpen Manse, Midlothian, Scotland. She was born about 1843 in Leith, Edinburgh, Scotland. She died on 30 Sep 1898 in Plattsburg, Wallsend, NSW, Australia.

More About Robert Smith:
Occupation: Coal Miner

More About Margaret Kerr:
Occupation: Paper Mill Worker

Robert Smith and Margaret Kerr had the following children:

     i.   WILLIAM[5] SMITH was born about 1865 in Loanhead, Midlothian, Scotland.

           More About William Smith:
           Occupation: Coal Miner

    ii.   HUNTER SMITH was born on 19 Dec 1866 in Lasswade, Midlothian, Scotland.

          More About Hunter Smith:
          Occupation: Coal Miner

    iii.   ANNIE KERR SMITH was born about 1869 in Lasswade, Midlothian, Scotland.

    iv.   EUPHEMIA BOWIE SMITH was born about 1871 in West Calder, Midlothian, Scotland. She died on 23 Feb 1945 in Wallsend, Australia.

    v.   ROBERT SMITH was born about 1874 in West Calder, Midlothian, Scotland.

    vi.   THOMAS SMITH was born about 1877 in Lasswade, Midlothian, Scotland.

    vii.   ALEXANDER BOWIE SMITH was born on 28 Dec 1878 in Lasswade, Midlothian, Scotland. He died on 25 Aug 1942 in Coledale, NSM, Australia.

    viii.   MARY ANN KERR SMITH was born about 1881 in Lasswade, Midlothian, Scotland. She died on 16 Sep 1941 in Lake MacQuarie, NSW, Australia.

30.   **HUNTER**[4] **SMITH** (Euphemia[3] Bowie, Hunter[2] Bowie, Robert[1] Bowie) was born about 1837 in Loanhead, Midlothian, Scotland. He died on 04 Oct 1914 in Wallsend, NSW, Australia. He married Agnes Lawson on 31 Dec 1858 in Barley Know, Scotland. She was born about 1837 in Barleydeen, Edinburgh, Scotland. She died on 30 Sep 1916 in Wallsend, NSW, Australia.

More About Hunter Smith:
Burial: 06 Oct 1914 in Presbyterian Cemetery, Wallsend, NSW, Australia
Occupation: Miner

Hunter Smith and Agnes Lawson had the following children:

    i.   AGNES[5] SMITH was born about 1862 in Loanhead, Lasswade, Midlothian, Scotland.

    ii.   EUPHEMIA I. SMITH was born in 1865. She died in 1867.

    iii.   WILLIAM R. SMITH was born about 1869.

    iv.   HUNTER BOWIE SMITH was born on 11 Apr 1871 in Plattburg, Newcastle, NSW, Australia. He died on 07 Jan 1966 in Wallsend, NSW, Australia.

    v.   CAROLINE SMITH was born about 1873.

31.   **JANE**[4] **BOWIE** (Robert[3], Hunter[2], Robert[1]) was born in 1849 in Cockpen, Midlothian, Scotland. She died on 16 Jan 1931 in Dalkeith, Midlothian, Scotland. She married (1) **JAMES DANIEL MILLER**, son of Robert Miller and Margaret McDonald on 31 Dec 1873 in Hunterfield, Midlothian, Scotland. He was born in 1851. He died on 21 May 1876 in Hunterfield, Midlothian, Scotland. She married (2) **JAMES KILGOUR DINGWALL**, son of Robert Dingwall and Elizabeth Kilgour on 20 Jul 1883 in Edinburgh, Scotland. He was born on 16 Apr 1843 in Strathmiglo, Perth, Scotland. He died on 04 Apr 1931 in Dalkeith, Midlothian, Scotland.

More About Jane Bowie:
Burial: 18 Jan 1931 in Dalkeith Cemetery, Dalkeith, Midlothian, Scotland

More About James Daniel Miller:
Occupation: Coal Miner

James Daniel Miller and Jane Bowie had the following children:

i. MARY JANE [5] MILLER was born on 13 Oct 1874 in Dalkeith, Midlothian, Scotland. She died on 04 Oct 1956. She married WILLIAM ROY. He was born in 1874. He died on 21 Dec 1930.

    More About Mary Jane Miller:
    Burial: Dalkeith Cemetery, Dalkeith, Midlothian, Scotland
    Occupation: Carpet Printer

ii. MARGARET MILLER was born in 1876 in Dalkeith, Midlothian, Scotland. She died about 1956.

More About James Kilgour Dingwall:
Burial: 07 Apr 1931 in Dalkeith Cemetery, Dalkeith, Midlothian, Scotland
Occupation: Railway Employee

James Kilgour Dingwall and Jane Bowie had the following children:

i. JAMES [5] DINGWALL was born on 26 May 1884 in Dalkeith, Midlothian, Scotland. He died on 01 Jul 1966 in Edinburgh, Scotland.

ii. MARION DINGWALL was born on 27 Jul 1885 in Dalkeith, Midlothian, Scotland. She died on 04 Oct 1975 in Liberton, Midlothian, Scotland. She married Nicholas Mason Whitehead Bethune on 07 Jun 1913 in Edinburgh, Scotland. He was born on 20 Jun 1886 in Lasswade, Midlothian, Scotland. He died on 30 Dec 1952 in Liberton, Midlothian, Scotland.

iii. THOMAS BOWIE DINGWALL was born in Dec 1886 in Dalkeith, Midlothian, Scotland. He died on 22 Aug 1917. He married CHARLOTTE BYERS.

    More About Thomas Bowie Dingwall:
    Military Service: Served with the Royal Scots in World War One

    Notes for Thomas Bowie Dingwall:
    Thomas Dingwall died while serving with the Royal Scots.

iv. GRACE MILLER DINGWALL was born on 15 Aug 1888 in Dalkeith, Midlothian, Scotland. She died in 1978 in Edinburgh, Midlothian, Scotland. She married John Herbert on 28 Dec 1923 in Dalkeith, Midlothian, Scotland. He was born in 1870. He died on 15 Sep 1947 in Edinburgh, Midlothian, Scotland.

v. ALEXANDER B. DINGWALL was born in Jul 1890 in Dalkeith, Midlothian, Scotland. He married EUPHEMIA BOWIE BROWN. She was born on 01 Apr 1890. She died on 12 Feb 1949.

vi. JOHN DINGWALL was born about 1892. He died in Mar 1893.

More About John Dingwall:
Burial: Dalkeith Cemetery, Dalkeith, Midlothian, Scotland

32.   **THOMAS YOUNG[4] BOWIE** (Robert[3], Hunter[2], Robert[1]) was born in 1853 in Cockpen, Midlothian, Scotland. He died on 31 Aug 1919. He married **ELIZABETH SMITH**. She was born in 1855. She died on 22 Feb 1934 in Dalkeith, Midlothian, Scotland.

More About Thomas Young Bowie:
Burial: 02 Sep 1919 in Dalkeith Cemetery, Dalkeith, Midlothian, Scotland
Occupation: Coal Miner

More About Elizabeth Smith:
Burial: 25 Feb 1934 in Dalkeith Cemetery, Dalkeith, Midlothian, Scotland

Thomas Young Bowie and Elizabeth Smith had the following children:

    i.   ELIZABETH[5] BOWIE.

    ii.   MARY BOWIE.

    iii.   ROBERT BOWIE.

        More About Robert Bowie:
        Occupation: Miner

    iv.   MARGARET SMITH BOWIE was born in 1883. She died in Mar 1954.

        More About Margaret Smith Bowie:
        Burial: Dalkeith Cemetery, Dalkeith, Midlothian, Scotland

    v.   WILLIAM BOWIE was born in May 1884.

    vi.   TOM BOWIE was born in 1889.

    vii.   JOHN BOWIE was born in 1893.

        More About John Bowie:
        Occupation: ; Joiner

    viii.   ALEX BOWIE was born in 1895.

    ix.   RICHARD BOWIE was born in 1897.

33.   **MARION[4] BOWIE** (Robert[3], Hunter[2], Robert[1]) was born on 16 Oct 1855 in Lasswade, Midlothian, Scotland. She died on 29 Jul 1936 in Bonnyrigg, Midlothian, Scotland. She married George Kerr Brown on 10 Jun 1881. He was born on 16 Aug 1855. He died on 29 Jun 1926 in Bonnyrigg, Midlothian, Scotland.

More About George Kerr Brown:
Occupation: Insurance Agent

Occupation: ; Justice of the Peace

George Kerr Brown and Marion Bowie had the following children:

    i.   MARY[5] BROWN was born on 16 Aug 1883.

    ii.   ISABELLA BROWN was born on 28 Apr 1884. She died on 18 Jan 1959.

    iii.   JEANIE BROWN was born on 05 Jan 1886. She died on 07 Aug 1886.

    iv.   ALEX BROWN was born on 22 Jan 1888.

    v.   EUPHEMIA BOWIE BROWN was born on 01 Apr 1890. She died on 12 Feb 1949. She married ALEXANDER B. DINGWALL. He was born in Jul 1890 in Dalkeith, Midlothian, Scotland.

        More About Euphemia Bowie Brown:
        Burial: 15 Feb 1949 in Dalkeith Cemetery, Dalkeith, Midlothian, Scotland

    vi.   ROBERT BOWIE BROWN was born on 10 Jan 1893. He died on 16 May 1952.

    vii.   GEORGE KERR BROWN was born on 12 Jan 1895.

34.   **RICHARD**[4] **BOWIE** (Robert[3], Hunter[2], Robert[1]) was born on 15 Dec 1863 in Newbattle, Midlothian, Scotland. He died on 22 Aug 1928. He married **ISABELLA BENNETT**. She was born in 1870. She died on 04 Mar 1967.

More About Richard Bowie:
Burial: Dalkeith Cemetery, Dalkeith, Midlothian, Scotland
Occupation: Gardener
Occupation: Coal Miner

More About Isabella Bennett:
Burial: Dalkeith Cemetery, Dalkeith, Midlothian, Scotland

Richard Bowie and Isabella Bennett had the following children:

    i.   ROBERT[5] BOWIE was born in 1893.

    ii.   ALEXANDER BENNETT BOWIE was born in 1895. He died on 18 Jan 1916 in France.

        More About Alexander Bennett Bowie:
        Burial: Quarry Cemetery, Vermelles, Pas de Calais, France
        Military Service: 5th Dragoon Guards (Trooper)

    iii.   ELLENA BOWIE was born in 1897. She died on 14 Feb 1977.

    iv.   THOMAS BOWIE was born in 1899. He died on 06 Sep 1918 in Flanders.

        More About Thomas Bowie:
        Burial: Hagle Dump Cemetery, Ieper, West-Viaanderen, Belgium
        Military Service: 12th Highland Light Infantry (Private)

     v.   JAMES BOWIE was born in 1901. He died on 15 Nov 1911.

       More About James Bowie:
       Burial: 17 Nov 1911 in Dalkeith Cemetery, Dalkeith, Midlothian, Scotland

     vi.   MARY BOWIE was born in 1903. She died in Dec 1965 in Canada.

     vii. RICHARD BOWIE was born in 1905.

     viii. ISABELLA BOWIE was born in 1909.

35.   **ELIZABETH YOUNG**[4] **BOWIE** (Robert[3], Hunter[2], Robert[1]) was born in 1871 in Cockpen, Midlothian, Scotland. She died on 21 Nov 1916. She married David W. Haggert on 31 Mar 1892 in Stobhill, Scotland. He died on 02 May 1955.

More About Elizabeth Young Bowie:
Burial: Dalkeith   Cemetery,   Dalkeith,   Midlothian,
Scotland
Occupation: Dressmaker

More About David W. Haggert:
Burial: Dalkeith Cemetery, Dalkeith, Midlothian, Scotland

David W. Haggert and Elizabeth Young Bowie had the following children:

     i.   MARY[5] HAGGERT was born on 29 Oct 1892 in Stobhill, Scotland.

     ii.   ELLA HAGGERT was born in 1895. She died on 26 Nov 1973. She married ALEX HARPER. He died on 29 Apr 1934.

       More About Ella Haggert:
       Burial: Dalkeith Cemetery, Dalkeith, Midlothian, Scotland

     iii. ANDREW BOWIE HAGGERT was born in 1898. He died on 11 Apr 1917 in France.

       Notes for Andrew Bowie Haggert:
       Wounded in the Battle of Arras and died from the wounds.

     iv. ROBERT HAGGERT. He married JEANIE SMALL.

     v.   WILLIAM HAGGERT was born on 08 Feb 1904. He married Henrietta Ann Lumsden Smith on 06 Aug 1941. She was born about 1919.

       More About William Haggert:
       Occupation: Grocer

     vi. JEAN HAGGERT.

36.   **HUNTER**[4] **BOWIE** (Robert[3], Euphemia[2], Robert[1]) was born in 1852 in Old Monkland, Lanarkshire, Scotland. He married Margaret Cameron, daughter of Alexander Cameron and Jean Adam on 21 Jul 1874 in Old Monkland, Lanarkshire, Scotland. She was born on 06 Jul 1851 in Old Monkland,

Lanarkshire, Scotland.

Hunter Bowie and Margaret Cameron had the following children:

<ol type="i">
<li>ROBERT[5] BOWIE was born in 1876 in Lugar, Ayrshire, Scotland.</li>
<li>JEAN BOWIE was born in 1877 in Lugar, Ayrshire, Scotland.</li>
<li>WILLIAM BOWIE was born in 1879 in Lugar, Ayrshire, Scotland.</li>
<li>HUNTER BOWIE was born in 1881 in Lugar, Ayrshire, Scotland. He married Janet Wardrope on 05 Jul 1906 in Old Cumnock, Ayrshire, Scotland. She was born in 1884 in Ayrshire, Scotland.</li>
<li>ALEXANDER BOWIE was born in 1883 in Auchinleck, Ayrshire, Scotland.</li>
<li>GEORGE C. BOWIE was born in 1885 in Auchinleck, Ayrshire, Scotland.</li>
<li>ANN C. BOWIE was born in 1888 in Auchinleck, Ayrshire, Scotland.</li>
<li>MARGARET BOWIE was born in 1890 in Auchinleck, Ayrshire, Scotland.</li>
<li>DONALD BOWIE was born in 1897 in Auchinleck, Ayrshire, Scotland.</li>
</ol>